W
& D
of Western Australia

by Carolyn Thomson

DEPARTMENT OF CONSERVATION AND LAND MANAGEMENT

INTRODUCTION

Whales and dolphins have long fascinated people. As well as being extremely graceful, they are also among the largest marine animals. They frequently show curiosity about us, too, and some species may come close to boats to investigate terrestrial intruders. Many people feel a special affinity with whales and dolphins, perhaps because, like us, they are air-breathing, warm-blooded mammals that nurse their young.

Some species are coastal in their habits. As a result, they often interact with people. The dolphins of Monkey Mia, at Shark Bay, are an example. In the 1960s, fisherfolk began feeding them when they returned with their catch. Over the years the tradition continued. News of the phenomenon travelled by word of mouth and visitors now come from far and wide to see the dolphins. They are wild animals that come to the beach of their own free will to interact with people and accept fish from them. Now all feeding is regulated by rangers to ensure the dolphins don't become too dependent on handouts.

Whales range in size and weight from the 31 metre blue whale, which is the world's largest living animal and weighs between 80 and 130 tonnes, to the 2.4 metre dwarf sperm whale, weighing about 150 kilograms. They are divided into **toothed** whales (such as sperm and killer whales) and **baleen** whales (such as humpbacks). Toothed whales feed on squid, fish and sometimes marine mammals. Baleen whales mostly sieve planktonic organisms from the water.

All whales and dolphins have smooth, streamlined bodies, lack external ears, have flippers like forelimbs for steering and manoeuvring, very few hairs and a layer of insulating blubber. These characteristics make them superbly adapted to the marine environment.

WHALE WATCHING

A code has been developed to encourage enjoyable and safe whale watching from boats, while protecting these giants from undue harassment.

Only approach a whale or group of whales from a direction parallel to them, and slightly to their rear. Alternatively, position your boat 300 metres ahead of them and allow the whales to approach you. Do not separate what may be members of a family group. If you are within 300 metres of a whale or whales, move the vessel at a consistently slow (no wake) speed. If you intend stopping the engines to watch, allow them to idle for a minute before switching off. Whales become alarmed at sudden noises, or at the sudden stopping of a noise they have grown used to.

Vessels should not approach closer than 100 metres to a whale. If an animal approaches the vessel more closely of its own accord, put the engine in neutral, and avoid using the propellers until it has moved off. Swimming with whales is not permitted. It may cause stress to the animal and is dangerous for people, as a tail or fluke slap can easily render a swimmer unconscious.

REMEMBER: If whales are diving for prolonged periods, or swimming evasively, you are disturbing and upsetting them - leave them alone. It is an offence to harass whales, and they may permanently abandon an area if they are continually disturbed.

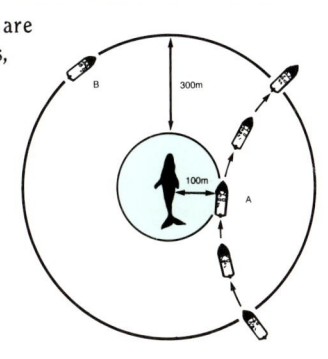

BEHAVIOUR

An adult humpback's two lungs, each the size of a small car, are emptied and refilled in less than two seconds. Contrary to the drawings on ancient maps, the whale does not blow a stream of water. As it surfaces, the humpback exhales through two blowholes on the top of its head. The air is expelled and cooled so rapidly it forms a distinctive cloud.

ROUND OUT

After inhaling through the blowhole, the humpback begins to dive by arching its body and rolling ahead. The name "humpback" comes from this regular action, which is called a "round out".

FLUKE UP/FLUKE DOWN DIVE

Raising the tail before diving may indicate the whale is about to make a steep descent into the sea and therefore dive for a prolonged period. In a fluke-up dive, the tail flukes are brought straight up in the air, exposing the whole lower surface, showing the unique markings found on each humpback. In a fluke-down dive, the flukes are brought clear of the water, but remain turned down.

PEC SLAP

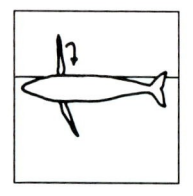

Humpbacks frequently roll at the surface, slapping their pectoral fins against the water.

TAIL SLAP

Tail slapping occurs while most of the animal is submerged and nearly vertical.

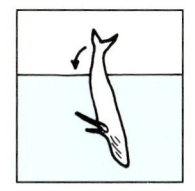

SPY HOP

Spy hopping occurs when the whale rises almost straight out of the water so its eyes clear the surface. It may then turn 90 to 180 degrees on its longitudinal axis, then slip back below the surface.

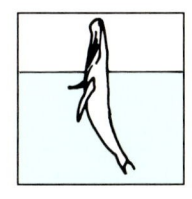

BREACH

The most spectacular behaviour is the breach. The whale propels most of its body from the water, then turns to crash back to the surface.

SOUTHERN RIGHT WHALE
(Eubalaena australis)

Southern right whales can often be seen by boaters, or sightseers watching from vantage points on land, at certain times of the year. Southern right whales are about the size of a bus. They weigh up to 80 tonnes and may reach 18 metres long. They also have the largest testes and penises of any living thing, with penises longer than 14 per cent of their body length. Although southern right whales are huge, bulky creatures, they are also agile and active animals, and their acrobatic antics can keep whale watchers amazed and entranced for hours. However, their commonest behaviour is lying around like logs at the surface.

DESCRIPTION: These mammals have horny growths called callosities on the top of their heads, behind their blowholes, on their chins, above their eyes and on their lower lips. Their exact function is unknown. The patterns formed by the callosities are different for each individual, and this has proved useful for researchers collecting information on patterns of movement and behaviour.

Southern right whales are large and stocky. The large head comprises up to a quarter of the total body length, and the lower jawline is distinctively bowed. There is no dorsal fin but they have broad, triangular and flat flippers. The body colour ranges from bluish-black to light brown but there are often white markings, usually on the belly. The twin blowholes produce a high, V-shaped blow. Albinos have been recorded but their colour becomes grey as the animals age, and they are therefore usually referred to as "partial" albinos. Southern right whales harbour large quantities of parasites (small crustaceans known as whale lice) and these are visible if you are close enough to the whale.

STATUS AND DISTRIBUTION: Southern right whales inhabit the cooler latitudes, where they were once abundant. They were the first large whale to be hunted by man, beginning in the tenth

7

century off Japan. Later on, these gentle giants were sought after by whalers for their oil and baleen. In fact, they were called right whales because in the days of open-boat whaling with hand harpoons they were the "right" ones to catch. They were slow-swimming, floated when dead, and yielded large amounts of valuable products - particularly oil for illumination and lubrication. More than 100,000 were caught in the nineteenth century alone. Populations declined to dangerously low levels even before the end of the nineteenth century. It is estimated that the entire world population of southern right whales now only numbers a few thousand, compared with an original population before whaling of more than 100,000. The population along the southern coast of Australia can be counted in the hundreds. Fortunately, it is now recovering at a rate of at least seven per cent each year, and the whales are once again becoming a spectacle along our coastline. However, they are still classed as endangered.

BEHAVIOUR: Southern right whales regularly engage in tail lobbing, flipper slapping and even head standing. After they breach, the sound of these mammoth acrobats hitting the water can be heard from a great distance. They are usually seen in mother and calf pairs, but occasionally congregate in groups of up to 20. These mammals may moan.

FEEDING: Right whales are baleen whales, which means they have horny plates of baleen hanging down from their upper jaws. They feed on swarms of plankton, which they sieve from the water through the fibrous inner hairs of the baleen plates. Most feeding is thought to occur in the highly productive polar areas during summer, but they do not move as far south as humpbacks or other baleen whales.

BREEDING: During summer, right whales prefer the open ocean, away from the coast, but during early winter and spring the cows come in close to shore. There, near the surf line in sheltered bays, they give birth to their young, before returning to deeper waters as summer approaches. On average, they calve once every three years. Newborn animals are between four and a half to six metres long and weigh approximately one and a half tonnes.

STRANDINGS: People often mistakenly believe southern right whales are stranding when they come in close to shore, but this is normal behaviour. However, they sometimes become entangled in nets. Examples are entanglements in Cockburn Sound in August 1992 and Warnbro Sound in August 1994. Right whales are powerful and it is difficult to get close to them without jeopardising human safety. However, because of the limited numbers of the species, it is especially important to rescue individuals in difficulty.

WHERE TO SEE THEM: Regular whale watching tours operate from Albany and Esperance in season. They can also be seen from vantage points along the shore, such as on the coast between Busselton and Augusta and at Point Ann, east of Bremer Bay, in the Fitzgerald National Park.

PYGMY RIGHT WHALE
(Caperea marginata)

Like southern right whales, pygmy right whales are baleen whales. They also share a strongly bowed lower jaw. Despite this superficial resemblance, they are not closely related and the pygmy right whale is in a family of its own. As well as being considerably smaller than the southern right whale, it has a more streamlined shape, a small dorsal fin and narrow flippers. It does not have callosities. This is the smallest of the baleen whales and individuals grow to about six metres long.

DESCRIPTION: The narrow, arched head of the pygmy right whale is smaller in proportion to the body than in other baleen whales. Their upper bodies and flippers are grey or black, with lighter colouring beneath. The tail flukes are broad and notched. Young animals are about three and a half metres long when they are weaned.

STATUS AND DISTRIBUTION: The pygmy right whale is found only in cool to temperate waters of the southern hemisphere. It only spends short periods at the surface, its dorsal fin is usually not visible and the blow is weak, so few animals have been recorded in the wild. Another difficulty is that at sea it strongly resembles the minke whale. The species was not exploited by people.

LIFE HISTORY: These whales are usually seen alone or in pairs. They feed on very small plankton, and their yellowish-white baleen is edged with very fine bristles. It has been surmised that they migrate inshore during spring and summer, sometimes moving into sheltered bays. In fact, one was photographed in Cockburn Sound in recent years - this was only the second time that a live pygmy right whale had been photographed in Australia.

STRANDINGS: Pygmy right whales are occasionally washed up dead on the WA coast between Fremantle and Albany.

11

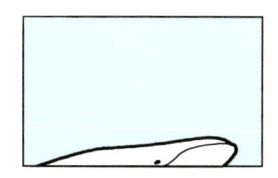

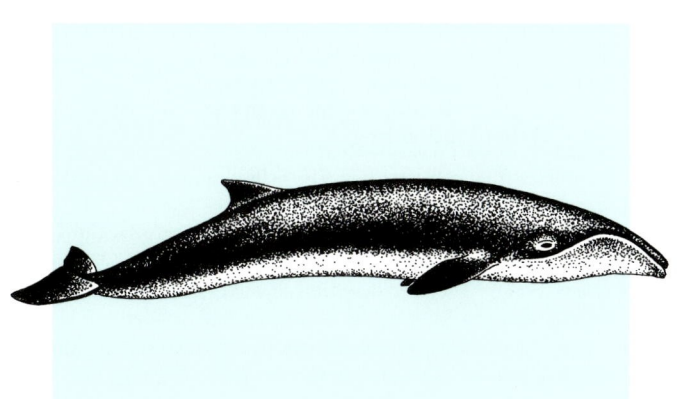

BLUE WHALE
(Balaenoptera musculus)

The blue whale is the largest living animal on Earth. Although the average length is 25 to 26 metres, females can reach more than 30 metres and weigh more than 160 tonnes at the end of the feeding season. Blue whales seen off WA are probably a subspecies known as the pygmy blue. However, the pygmy blue is only marginally shorter than the true blue whale.

DESCRIPTION: The huge size, mottled bluish-grey colour and small stubby dorsal fin positioned well back on the body distinguish blue whales from other whales. The belly assumes a yellowish-brown colour after they have been living in polar areas for a while, as a result of microscopic algae known as diatoms growing on their skin. When viewed from the air, their streamlined, slender shape is obvious. They also have a broad, flat U-shaped head, with a central ridge in front of the blowholes, and slender pointed flippers. Their blow is vertical and may be nine metres high. The large, notched tail flukes are sometimes raised when they dive.

STATUS AND DISTRIBUTION: The population has been severely depleted by whaling, with nearly 30,000 caught in one season alone. The southern hemisphere population is estimated at less than 20,000, representing only a fraction of what it was in pre-whaling days. Blue whales are rarely seen near the WA coast, but have been seen offshore from Rottnest Island.

MIGRATION: Blue whales cover thousands of kilometres each year, migrating between subtropical or tropical waters, where they give birth in winter, and polar regions, which are the most productive areas for feeding, in summer. Pregnant females are usually the first to arrive in polar waters, and the last to leave.

LIFE HISTORY: Calves are about seven metres long and two and a half tonnes at birth. By the time they are weaned, seven or eight months later, they are almost 15 metres long. They are usually solitary or seen in pairs, but may be found in larger groups in feeding areas. The species feeds principally on dense swarms of krill (tiny shrimp-like crustaceans) taken near the surface and probably do not dive deeply. Blue whales may live an impressive 80 years or more. Sharks and killer whales may attack and kill young, wounded or diseased animals. They make low frequency moans, pulses and buzzes. Ultrasonic clicks are probably used for echolocation.

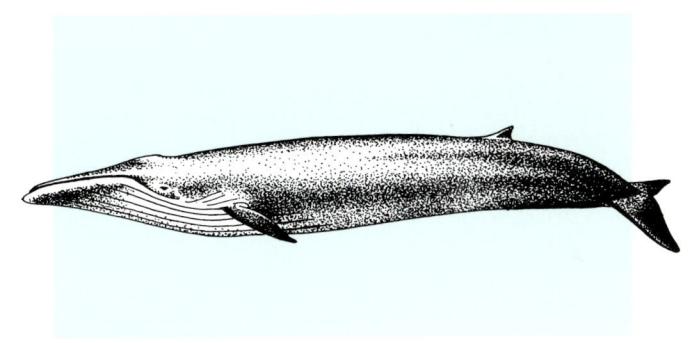

BRYDE'S WHALE
(Balaenoptera edeni)

Bryde's whales were among the sea creatures that amazed the public and marine biologists when they were filmed in June 1993, taking part in an incredible feeding frenzy at Cape Cuvier, on the WA coast near Carnarvon. The whales, mouths agape and baleen exposed, were seen lunging through massive swarms of anchovies that had become trapped against the cliffs by a number of whales, sharks and other predators. The feeding frenzy continued for weeks and is now believed to be a regular occurrence at this time of the year. Bryde's (pronounced "broodahs") whales engage in spectacular behaviour such as breaching clear of the water.

DESCRIPTION: Bryde's whales are distinguished by the three ridges on top of their quite slender bodies, which run from the front of the head to the blowholes. Adults may reach up to 14 metres, with females slightly larger than males. Other features include broad, notched tail flukes, pointed flippers and a dorsal fin about two-thirds back along their bodies. They are dark grey on their upper bodies, with white patches on the chin and throat. The blow rises in a cloud three to four metres high.

STATUS AND DISTRIBUTION: In WA these mammals are found from Shark Bay northwards and range through all the world's warm temperate, subtropical and tropical waters. They were hunted systematically in the North Pacific and off Peru, but very little anywhere else. On the whole, the species is not considered to be significantly depleted.

LIFE HISTORY: Bryde's whales may live for 50 years or more. They are mostly seen alone or in pairs, unless a number arrive to gorge on an abundance of food as described above. Some individuals inhabit coastal waters, while others live offshore. They give birth to a single calf every two years or so. Some forms may breed at any time throughout the year, while others breed seasonally. Their movements seem to be influenced mostly by the availability of food, which consists of small shoaling fish or swarming plankton. They tend to move east-west rather than north-south.

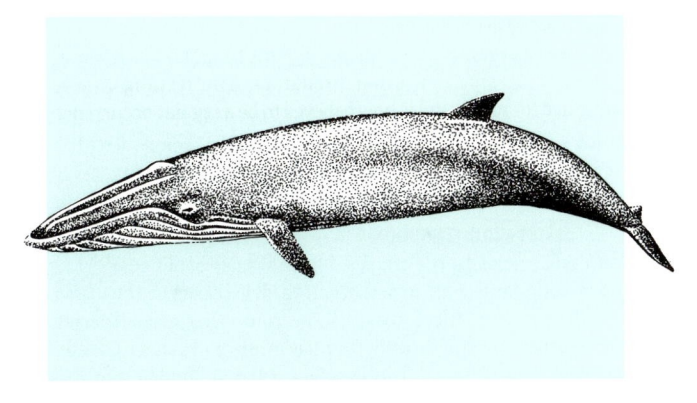

MINKE WHALE
(Balaenoptera acutostrata)

Abundant in all the world's oceans, these inquisitive whales often breach and engage in spy hopping. They sometimes approach boats. Like blue whales, Bryde's whales and humpbacks, minke whales have pleated throats that allow them to take in large quantities of water, from which they strain small shoaling fish or plankton.

DESCRIPTION: The most distinctive feature of this baleen whale is the narrow, sharply triangular head on which there is a single raised ridge. The colouring is dark bluish-grey above. The pleated throat and other underparts are lighter and the average length is eight metres. Minke whales arch their backs while diving but do not raise their tail flukes. Their blows are about two to three metres high.

STATUS AND DISTRIBUTION: These widespread animals are found from polar areas to the tropics. Minke whales could possibly be more abundant than in pre-whaling days because they have benefited from reduced competition from other whale species. The species was traditionally hunted in places such as Canada, Scandinavia and Japan. The Japanese still take limited numbers of minke whales under scientific permit.

LIFE HISTORY: They may live up to 60 years. They give birth to a single calf, approximately two and a half metres long, in winter. Minke whales are found alone or in groups of two or three.

STRANDING HISTORY: Minke whales often strand, usually singly.

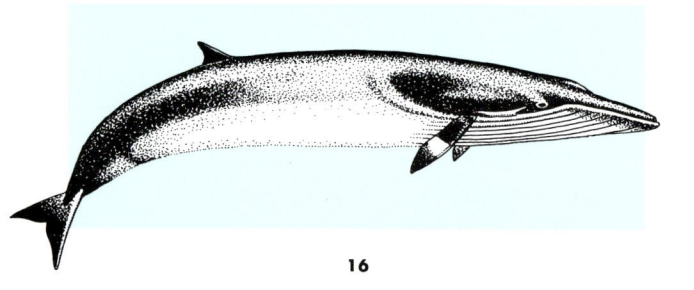

HUMPBACK WHALE
(*Megaptera novaeangliae*)

Humpbacks are the fifth largest of the great whales and are noted for their haunting songs. Named because of the distinct "hump" that shows as the whale arches its back when it dives, humpbacks are more coastal than most of the other large baleen whales. When in a playful mood, they may put on spectacular displays: breaching, rolling, slapping their pectoral fins and generally having a "whale" of a time.

DESCRIPTION: Humpbacks have knobby heads, very long flippers with knobs on the front edge, and a humped dorsal fin. They are blackish, with white undersides and sides. Males average 14.6 metres and females 15.2 metres long. The maximum length is 18 metres and a mature adult may weigh up to 45 tonnes.

STATUS AND DISTRIBUTION: Humpbacks are widely distributed throughout all the world's oceans. They were heavily exploited by whalers and their numbers were severely depleted. The population has been recovering at a remarkable 10 per cent each year since they became protected in 1963. Nevertheless, there are estimated to be only a few thousand humpback whales in southern oceans and in WA they are considered endangered.

MIGRATION: Each autumn, in late April to early May, the Australian humpbacks leave Antarctica to migrate northwards to their tropical calving grounds along the west and east coasts of Australia. About August, they begin travelling south to their feeding grounds in the Antarctic, so they can be seen passing through Perth waters from September to November, peaking in October. The first animals to be seen heading south are usually the newly pregnant females, followed by the immature whales of both sexes, then the mature males and females. Mothers with newborn calves stay longest, and travel more slowly, enabling the calves to grow rapidly and develop a thicker layer of blubber for protection in the cold feeding waters they will soon be visiting for the first time.

FEEDING: Australia's humpback whales spend the summer in the waters of Antarctica feeding mainly on krill. They are filter feeders, straining their food from the water by means of hundreds of horny baleen plates hanging from their upper jaws. These have bristly edges which mesh to form a filter. Humpbacks can consume nearly one tonne of food each day. They feed where large concentrations of prey are available.

BREEDING: When they are born, after about a 12 month gestation period, calves are about four and a half metres long and weigh about one and a half tonnes. The mother's milk has a 35 per cent fat content and milk production can be as high as 600 litres per day. The sucking calf can gain more than 45 kilograms a day during the first few weeks of life. Nursing ends at about 11 months, when the calf can be up to nine metres long.

STRANDING HISTORY: They rarely strand. However, a humpback yearling stranded at Bunbury in October 1990 and had to be euthanased by implosion. There is little rescuers can do to help humpbacks, as these huge animals are impossible to move.

WHERE TO SEE THEM: Following their recovery from the brink of extinction, pods of humpbacks are once again becoming a spectacle as they pass close to the WA coast on their journey south. In the north-west they pass the Dampier Archipelago near Karratha and marine parks at Ningaloo and Marmion. They can also be seen off the Leeuwin-Naturaliste coast and Albany. Regular whale watching tours operate from Perth, Busselton and Dunsborough in season. They are inexpensive and highly recommended.

19

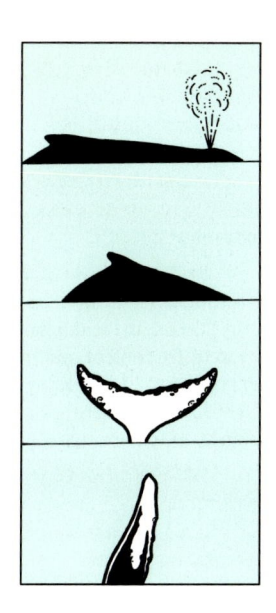

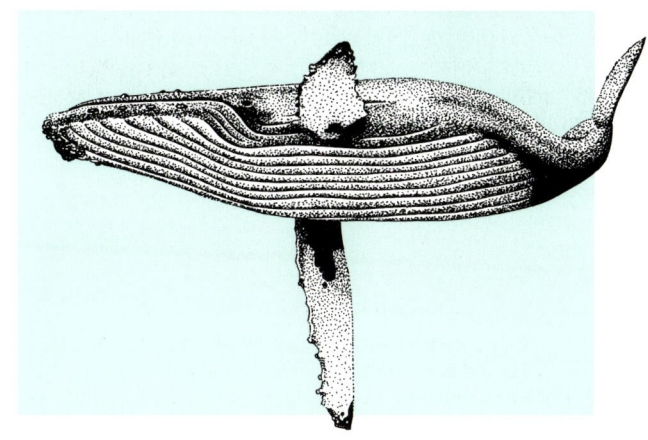

SPERM WHALE
(Physeter macrocephalus)

Sperm whales are truly majestic animals. They are the largest of the toothed whales and can grow to more than 18 metres long and weigh up to 60 tonnes. The name *macrocephalus* means "big head", which is indeed appropriate since the head is a quarter of the body length in calves and, with age, may form more than a third of the length of the body. The common name of sperm whale was given because whalers thought the liquid substance in its head resembled the fluid produced by the testes. This may be an important aid in its ability to dive to tremendous depths. It has been surmised that the sperm whale may be able to change the density of the spermaceti and therefore control the buoyancy of its body. These large animals are found relatively close to the mainland in the Albany area, which was the reason for the existence of the former Cheyne Beach Whaling Station at Albany. In future, it is possible that a sperm whale-watching industry could build up offshore from Albany.

DESCRIPTION: Sperm whales are easily recognised by the rectangular head shown in drawings of Moby Dick. Their cylindrical lower jaws contain rows of huge teeth that may weigh more than a kilogram each. They have dark grey or dark brown bodies and the heads of the males may be heavily scarred as a result of fights with other bulls or with giant squid, which they eat. The average length of this species is around 15 metres in males and 11 metres in females. The flippers are short and stubby but the tails are large and powerful and the flukes triangular in shape. In the ocean sperm whales are usually located by their bushy, five metre high blows. The blowhole is on the left of the head and the blow is lopsided and projects forward.

STATUS AND DISTRIBUTION: They range from the Equator to the North and South Poles in waters at least 180 metres deep. These whales were hunted for their oil and spermaceti. Ambergris,

21

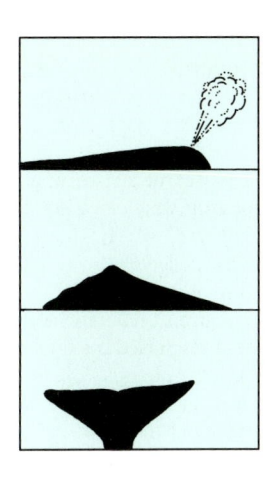

a fragrant waxy substance in the gut that forms around squid beaks, was used in the perfume industry. Despite being hunted for more than 300 years, the sperm whale remains reasonably abundant.

LIFE HISTORY: Sperm whales are probably the longest and deepest divers of all whales and dolphins. Dives may last more than 90 minutes and be to depths up to 2800 metres, and possibly deeper. They often raise their tail flukes before diving. These oceanic animals are rarely seen near shore, unless sick. During their seasonal movements, between the colder areas in summer and warmer zones in winter, they may travel for thousands of kilometres. Females and their offspring live in family groups of between 10 and 20 animals, within which they usually spend their whole lives. The adult males live in separate "bachelor pods". Groups of hundreds have been seen travelling together. Sperm whales vocalise in clicks. Certain click sequences, known as codas, have been recorded and these probably convey messages to other whales.

BREEDING: This species is long-lived and reproduces at an extremely low rate. Females become sexually mature at between eight and 11 years of age. They calve after a lengthy gestation period (14 to 15.5 months), at intervals of between three and 15 years. The calves are about four metres long at birth. They begin to eat solids in their first year but may continue to suckle until about 10 years of age. Because the bulls have to compete for access to females, they may have to wait until they are more than 20 years of age before they can mate. There are stories from whalers telling of great fights between bulls, sometimes resulting in severe injuries. The bulls continue to get bigger and more solitary as they age.

FEEDING: Sperm whales feed all year round on squid, octopuses and sometimes fish and may hunt in lines. Food is taken in mid-water, usually below 400 metres, and the whales may also feed on the bottom. As no sunlight can penetrate these depths, they are thought to locate their food by echolocation.

PYGMY SPERM WHALE
(Kogia breviceps)

These slow-moving mammals are found in temperate, tropical and subtropical seas.

DESCRIPTION: Reaching a maximum length of little more than three metres, they have a relatively short head with a narrow, underslung mouth beneath a bulbous snout. The snout, which contains the spermaceti organ, is pointed in young animals but becomes rectangular with age. Like the sperm whale, the blowhole is positioned on the top left hand side of the head. Pygmy sperm whales also have a small, hooked dorsal fin and broad tail flukes. Their upper half is dark bluish-grey, graduating to pinkish off-white on the underside. A distinguishing feature is the light, bracket-shaped marking on each side of the head, which is sometimes referred to as a "false gill". Males and females are a similar size.

LIFE HISTORY: The species is oceanic and thought to reside seaward of the continental slope, with females and their young possibly moving on to the continental shelf to feed. Pygmy sperm whales consume oceanic squid and cuttlefish, along with small amounts of fish or deep sea shrimp. These whales have been exploited in low numbers in the past. Single animals or mother-calf pairs occasionally strand, but may be misidentified as sharks because of the shape of the head.

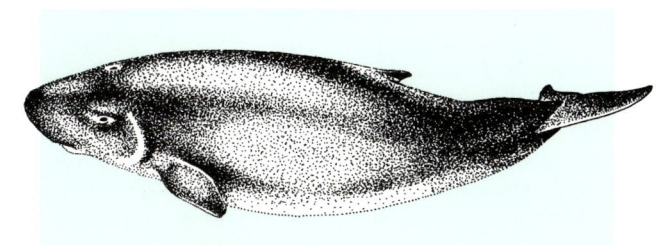

DWARF SPERM WHALE
(Kogia simus)

It's a case of dwarf by name and dwarf by nature. These are the smallest of all the whales and they have a snubbed squarish snout. They look very much like pygmy sperm whales.

DESCRIPTION: The dorsal fin is tall and broad at the base and its shape resembles that of many dolphin species. The maximum length they attain is 2.7 metres.

LIFE HISTORY: Gestation is nine months and newborn calves are about a metre long. They forage in groups of 10 or less, taking a variety of small prey such as tiny cuttlefish at depths of more than 250 metres.

STATUS AND DISTRIBUTION: Dwarf sperm whales are found throughout tropical, subtropical and temperate seas in both hemispheres. The species has been hunted in the past, probably in low numbers, and they may be caught incidentally in gillnets.

STRANDING HISTORY: They do strand on occasion. Stranded animals taken to marine parks to be rehabilitated have not survived for more than a few days.

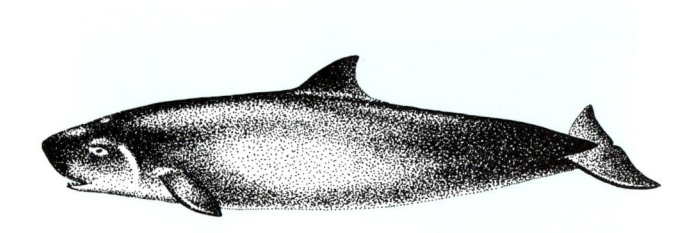

ARNOUX'S BEAKED WHALE
(Berardius arnouxii)

Living in deep, offshore waters south of the Tropic of Capricorn, Arnoux's beaked whales are rarely recorded in WA waters. They usually associate in groups of between six to 10 individuals, but up to 80 have been seen together.

DESCRIPTION: They have dark grey bodies above and lighter colouring below, and males tend to be heavily scarred. Arnoux's beaked whales have a prominent melon and a large beak with the lower jaw longer than the upper jaw. Mature males and females have two pairs of teeth near the tip. They may reach slightly less than 10 metres long. At sea, these deep divers are difficult to distinguish from the southern bottlenose whale and Baird's beaked whale.

LIFE HISTORY: They are thought to feed on squid and other deep sea creatures. Little is known about them.

SOUTHERN BOTTLENOSE WHALE
(Hyperoodon planifrons)

Southern bottlenose whales can be distinguished by their bulbous, and sometimes overhanging, melons. They dive deeply for their main prey of squid and the melon is probably an important aid in echolocation. They are able to remain below for more than an hour.

DESCRIPTION: Bottlenose whales have a relatively small head and beak compared to their elongated light brown or dull yellow bodies, which may reach up to eight metres long. Males have a pair of teeth at the tip of the snout. The head is a paler colour and larger animals are quite scarred. These mammals also have a slight depression near the blowhole and the dorsal fin is positioned towards the rear of the body.

STATUS AND DISTRIBUTION: Southern bottlenose whales are found throughout the southern oceans and the Antarctic. They have not been commercially exploited and are reasonably abundant.

LIFE HISTORY: They live in groups of up to 25, although the number is more likely to be less than 10, and are thought to calve in spring.

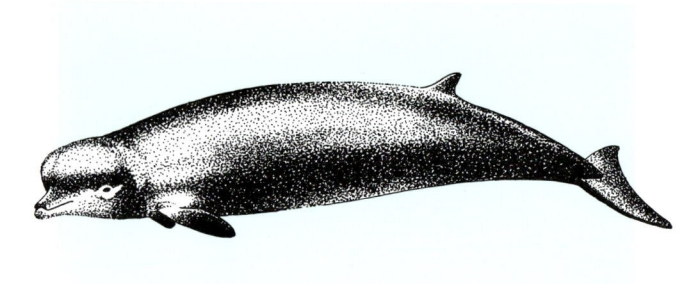

CUVIER'S BEAKED WHALE
(Ziphius cavirostris)

Cuvier's beaked whale is also called the goose-beaked whale because of the shape of its head and beak. In Japan it is called *akabo-kujira*, which means "baby-faced whale". The mouth is curved at the back and seems to be smiling, and the beak is not well defined from the melon.

DESCRIPTION: The flippers are small and males have two teeth at the tip of the lower jaw. Colour and markings vary considerably between individuals. These animals are usually between five to six metres long.

STATUS AND DISTRIBUTION: Cuvier's beaked whales are wide-ranging and abundant, being present in all but polar seas. They are not thought to be migratory. Small numbers are fished in Japan and elsewhere.

LIFE HISTORY: These mammals inhabit deep water and rarely approach the coast. They feed on deep sea fish and squid and may dive for 30 minutes or more. This, together with their inconspicuous blows, means they are rarely seen. Cuvier's beaked whales may live to at least 35 years, but probably survive longer. They usually form small groups of three to 10, although adult males tend to be solitary. Most strandings are of single animals.

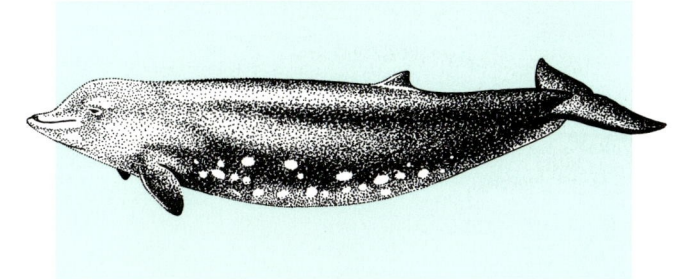

SHEPHERD'S BEAKED WHALE
(Tasmacetus shepherdi)

Shepherd's beaked whales are thought to live well away from the coast, and they are rarely seen alive. The species inhabits cold and temperate southern oceans and dead animals are occasionally found in New Zealand and elsewhere.

DESCRIPTION: The beak is longer and more pointed than those of most other beaked whales, with numerous teeth on the upper and lower jaws, and the animal has a fairly steep forehead. Other physical characteristics include a small dorsal fin and flippers and a stripe from the back of the flippers to the genitals. The upper body is dark with light undersides and there is no notch between the tail flukes. The males also have tusks at the front of their lower jaws. This species grows to a maximum length of seven metres.

LIFE HISTORY: Shepherd's beaked whales are believed to feed on fish at the bottom and in fairly deep water, so they are thought to be deep divers.

STRANDING HISTORY: Three Shepherd's beaked whales stranded near Busselton in January 1989.

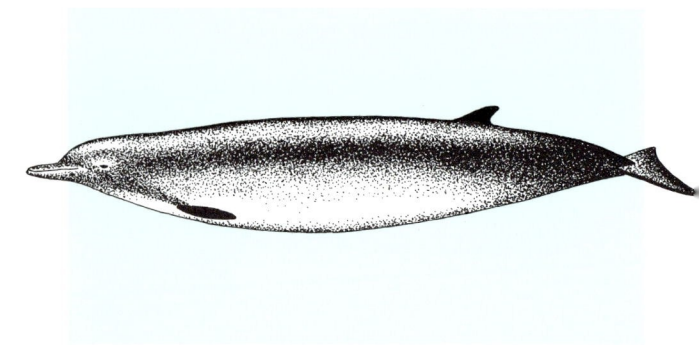

BLAINVILLE'S BEAKED WHALE
(Mesoplodon densirostris)

Blainville's beaked whales can be recognised by the unusual shape of their lower jaws, which are raised in an arch. A huge forward-tilting tooth grows on the peak of this arch and in males it may be higher than the forehead and covered in barnacles. Because bone specimens are said to be extraordinarily heavy, the species is also commonly known as the dense-beaked whale.

DESCRIPTION: Adults grow to a maximum length of up to five metres. They are dark bluish-grey on their upper bodies and paler below. Lighter blotches, scars and scratches often cover the body. Females appear to develop white jaws and calves are lighter in colour.

STATUS AND DISTRIBUTION: This is the most widely distributed of all the *Mesoplodon* species, being found in all temperate, tropical and subtropical areas. Scars suggest that they may be attacked by killer whales or false killer whales. In the past, small numbers have also been harpooned by people.

LIFE HISTORY: The species lives in pods of between three and seven and is thought to feed on squid and possibly some fish.

STRANDING HISTORY: A male Blainville's beaked whale was found dead at Two Rocks, north of Perth, in November 1990. This was the first recorded stranding in WA. The cause of death was unknown.

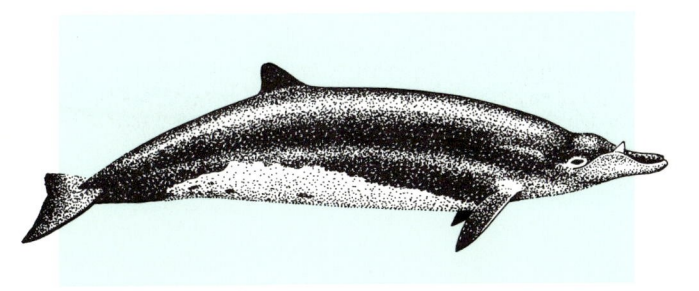

TRUE'S BEAKED WHALE
(Mesoplodon mirus)

True's beaked whales inhabit temperate waters in both hemispheres, but appear to be absent from polar and tropical waters. Little is known about them, although they occasionally strand on the southern coast of Australia.

DESCRIPTION: Scratches and scars mark their bodies, which are a greyish-black colour, with a white area extending back from the dorsal fin. The sides and belly are a lighter shade of grey. Adults are approximately five metres long and those found in the southern hemisphere also have a white beak tip. In males, two very small teeth protrude from the tip of the lower jaw.

STRANDING HISTORY: The main food source of True's beaked whales is thought to be squid.

STRAPTOOTHED WHALE
(Mesoplodon layardii)

This beaked whale derives its name from the bizarre, strap-like teeth found in adult males. The tips grow up and back, until they almost meet outside the beak above the upper jaw. In fact, the jaw is unable to fully open, but the whale is still able to feed. The teeth are absent in young animals and females.

DESCRIPTION: The whales also have a small melon-like bulge in front of the blowhole, and a white beak and throat. Otherwise they are mostly black, except for a grey blaze between the melon and the dorsal fin and a white oval near the genitals. Straptoothed whales are usually five to six metres long.

STATUS AND DISTRIBUTION: This oceanic species is relatively common in cool and temperate regions of the southern hemisphere, especially Australian and New Zealand waters.

STRANDING HISTORY: Straptoothed whales strand fairly frequently.

SCAMPERDOWN WHALE
(Mesoplodon grayi)

The scamperdown whale has a long, narrow beak that becomes white with maturity. Its head is small and the lower jaw of the male has two small triangular teeth near the middle of the beak.

DESCRIPTION: This mammal's average length is about five metres. The body is dark bluish-grey or brownish-grey above and somewhat lighter below, and there are often numerous scars and spots on the body.

STATUS AND DISTRIBUTION: Scamperdown whales are relatively common in the cool, temperate waters of the southern hemisphere, especially around Australia and New Zealand.

STRANDING HISTORY: The species strands frequently. A scamperdown whale that stranded at Dunsborough in December 1989 was successfully returned to the ocean, the first time this species is known to have been rescued anywhere in the world. The social structure of this species has some degree of cohesion, as more than one animal may become stranded.

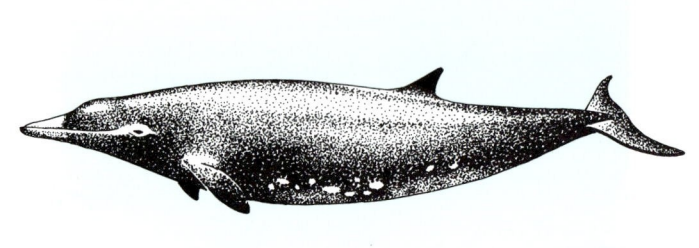

ANDREW'S BEAKED WHALE
(Mesoplodon bowdoini)

Very little is known about Andrew's beaked whale, which appears to be found only in the southern Indian and Pacific Oceans.

DESCRIPTION: The scientific name *Mesoplodon* is a combination of three Greek words that mean "having a tooth in the middle of the jaw", and males have two massive teeth protruding from either side of their arched lower jaw. Andrew's beaked whales are generally between four and five metres long and have a white, quite short beak and a dark, bluish-black body, with a smattering of scars.

LIFE HISTORY: The species is believed to breed in spring.

STRANDING HISTORY: Andrew's beaked whale has stranded on the southern coast of Australia, in New Zealand and on a sub-Antarctic island, but such occurrences are rare.

MELON-HEADED WHALE
(Peponocephala electra)

Melon-headed whales are highly social and generally roam in pods of 100 to 500 or more. They are rapid swimmers when excited and sometimes associate with dolphins. They frequently strand en masse.

DESCRIPTION: This small and little-known species has a melon-like head, though it is quite pointed at the tip. Melon-headed whales have a high dorsal fin halfway along their slender bodies, which are very dark in colour, apart from white lips and some pale patches on the undersides. They reach a maximum length of 2.8 metres. The flippers are fairly long, curved and pointed and the tail flukes are notched. At sea they are easily confused with pygmy killer whales and false killer whales, but on the beach their numerous teeth distinguish them from other whales with a similar appearance.

STATUS AND DISTRIBUTION: Melon-headed whales are found in tropical, subtropical and warm temperate waters. Although no estimate of the world population of these whales is available, they are not thought to be common.

LIFE HISTORY: These mammals feed primarily on squid and small fish. The species calves between August and December and no migrations are known.

PYGMY KILLER WHALE
(Feresa attenuata)

The pygmy killer whale is widely distributed but by no means abundant, inhabiting oceanic waters in all tropical and subtropical areas. Despite its small size - it is less than three metres long - it is aggressive and sometimes preys on other whales and dolphins. The bulk of its diet, however, is formed of squid and fish, including dolphinfish.

DESCRIPTION: The species is dark grey, brownish-grey or bluish-black, with a darker stripe from the top of the head that widens to a saddle around the dorsal fin. It also has a high, pointed dorsal fin and reasonably long flippers, which are rounded at the tip. There are usually white lips and a white patch on the belly.

LIFE HISTORY: Pygmy killer whales live in groups of up to 50, but several hundred are sometimes seen together. They may engage in playful behaviour, such as leaping, spy hopping and bow riding. Whistles, clicks and growls have been recorded from mammals kept in captivity. In some parts of the world they are frequently killed in fishery entrapments.

FALSE KILLER WHALE
(*Pseudorca crassidens*)

False killer whales are best known in WA from two dramatic mass strandings at Augusta in 1986 and 1988. Footage of them being successfully rescued was beamed all around the world.

DESCRIPTION: This medium-sized whale has a long, slender body and a narrow, tapered head with a rounded snout. Its dorsal fin is high and curved and the narrow, tapered flippers have a distinct hump or elbow on the front edge. The false killer whale is black with a grey chest, and the sides of the head are sometimes light grey. Average length is 4.6 metres for females and 5.4 metres for males. Calves are about one and a half metres at birth.

STATUS AND DISTRIBUTION: False killer whales are found worldwide, in all tropical and temperate seas. They are sometimes seen close to the coast in cooler waters, but tend to be oceanic, rarely approaching land unless there is deep water nearby. They often form herds of more than 100 individuals of both sexes and all age groups and appear to have strong social cohesion. They are occasionally driven ashore in Japan and eaten and are sometimes drowned in drift nets.

LIFE HISTORY: False killer whales are playful and readily bow ride, sometimes leaping right into the air. They thrive on squid and large fish and may attack groups of small dolphins. These mammals breed all year round and are thought to have a long gestation period. They are not known to be migratory.

STRANDING HISTORY: Large herds of false killer whales sometimes strand themselves dramatically on a beach. In 1986, 114 false killer whales stranded en masse at Augusta: 96 were successfully returned to the sea. In 1988 another large pod of false killer whales were stranded near Augusta. Thirty-two of them were returned to the sea, but a separate mass stranding of 24 whales about 30 kilometres east of Augusta was discovered too late and 16 had to be euthanased.

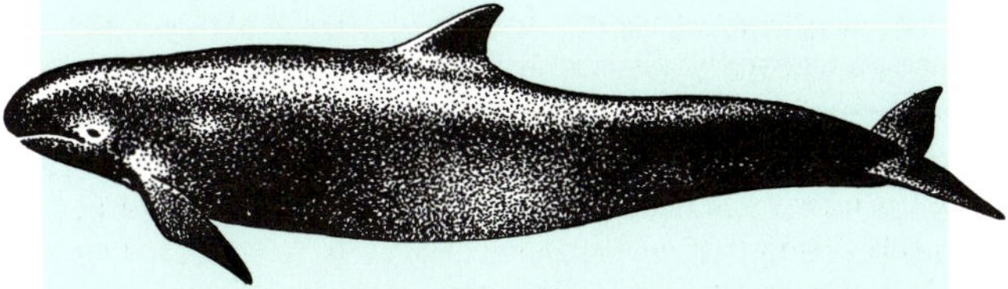

KILLER WHALE
(Orcinus orca)

The name *orca* is Latin for "demon". This and the term "killer whale" is no doubt derived from its liking for warm-blooded prey. It will attack animals of all sizes, even the massive blue whale. Dolphins, seals, dugongs, turtles, penguins and a variety of birds, fish and other whales are also included on the menu. Despite being the second largest toothed whale (only the sperm whale is larger), it is more closely related to dolphins than to most other whale species. Unlike some other parts of the world, groups of killer whales do not occupy defined home ranges off the WA coast. However, they are seasonal visitors and often follow migrating humpback whales to pick off the calves and old animals. Pods frequently enter Shark Bay to hunt dugongs.

DESCRIPTION: Killer whales are picturesque and well known to most people from photographs, films and captive animals at oceanariums. Their stocky black and white bodies are strikingly patterned. The dorsal fins are extraordinarily high, especially the straight fins of males, which may be up to 1.8 metres tall. Females have shorter and more dolphin-like fins. They also have quite large, broad flippers. These mammals have rounded heads with indistinct beaks and their mouths have dangerous-looking teeth suitable for tearing up large prey. Average length is between six and eight metres. Males are generally larger than females and may reach more than nine metres. Newborn calves are between two and two and a half metres long.

STATUS AND DISTRIBUTION: They are one of the most wide-ranging of all the whale species - found from the Equator to the icy polar regions, and from the coast to the deepest parts of all the world's oceans. They may also enter estuaries. The species is quite abundant despite being hunted by whalers, captured for oceanariums and culled by fishermen in certain areas.

Right: *The dorsal fin of the male killer whale (top) is taller and straighter than that of the female (centre).*

LIFE HISTORY: Killer whales live in pods of between two and 40. Each group includes at least one large male. They may hunt in packs and share their catches with others in the group in a similar manner to lions. Their social behaviour is fascinating. There is thought to be a pecking order to maintain stability. Members of the group communicate by means of pulses, clicks, whistles and scream-like noises, particularly when hunting. They frequently breach, spy hop and slap their tails, but their blows are low and bushy. The species may live up to 90 years, but mortality is usually about 30 years in males and 50 years in females.

LONG-FINNED PILOT WHALE
(Globicephala melas)

What's in a name? In the case of the long-finned pilot whale, a great deal. *Globicephala* means "globe-head" in Latin (in some places the species is unkindly referred to as the pothead whale) and *melas* means "black". It is probably known as the pilot whale because of its reputation for piloting fishermen towards schools of fish.

DESCRIPTION: These whales are brownish-grey to black, apart from a pinkish anchor shape on the undersides. They are also distinguished by a high, bulbous forehead and the long, sickle-shaped flippers pointed on the tip are at least a fifth of the body length. They have a distinct dorsal fin which is low and longer at the base than at the peak. These mammals usually have a grey saddle patch on their back, and a grey streak behind the eyes. The maximum length is six and a half metres, with males larger than females. Calves are less than two metres long at birth. The short-finned pilot whale looks very similar to this species.

STATUS AND DISTRIBUTION: The long-finned pilot whale is abundant and widely distributed in the cold temperate waters of the southern hemisphere and North Atlantic. It feeds largely on squid, and the movements of these abundant invertebrates probably determine the daily activities and seasonal movements of pilot whales. The species was hunted for centuries in the North Atlantic for its meat and oil.

LIFE HISTORY: This species may be able to dive to hundreds of metres to obtain food. Its normal lifespan is between 30 and 50 years, with calves born every three to four years. Pilot whales are essentially oceanic. The males have fighting scars, so probably compete for females, and they also have a higher mortality rate than females. These mammals are thought to navigate by means of clicks and communicate by whistling. They live in groups of tens or hundreds and often associate with species such as minke whales or bottlenose dolphins.

STRANDING HISTORY: Pilot whale strandings are common throughout the world. They tend to strand, both individually and in herds from several hundred to more than 1000. A baby pilot whale stranded in 1989 near Lancelin. Rescuers tried to keep it alive but it died after a few days. Fifty-four pilot whales stranded at Parrys Inlet, between Walpole and Albany, in 1971 and 18 stranded at Point Charles, in the Fitzgerald National Park, in 1979.

SHORT-FINNED PILOT WHALE
(*Globicephala macrorhynchus*)

Short-finned pilot whales are closely related to long-finned pilot whales, although they have shorter flippers with less of an elbow. They may swim side by side in formations known as "chorus lines" up to four kilometres across.

DESCRIPTION: Like long-finned pilot whales, short-finned pilot whales are brownish-grey to black, with a pinkish-grey anchor shape on the undersides. They have a similar bulbous forehead but the flippers are less than 18 per cent of the body length. There is usually a grey saddle patch on the back, and a grey streak behind the eyes. Females are about four metres long and males approximately five and a half metres. Newborn calves are about one and a half metres long.

STATUS AND DISTRIBUTION: These mammals inhabit tropical and subtropical waters. Short-finned pilot whales have been deliberately hunted or accidentally entangled since the nineteenth century, but not as intensively as some other whale species. They are believed to be reasonably abundant.

LIFE HISTORY: They may be seen in the hundreds but groups usually number less than 100. Short-finned pilot whales also associate with other whale and dolphin species and eat octopuses, squid and, to a lesser extent, fish. They may live to more than 60 years of age. Females may produce milk long after they have their last calf at about 37 years, and may then suckle other calves in the group.

STRANDING HISTORY: They often strand en masse. Nine short-finned pilot whales were found dead after stranding at Albany's Ledge Point in November 1984. Thirty eight pilot whales stranded in April 1991 at Sandy Point, north of Broome, but died within a few hours. Nine whales that stranded at nearby Lombardina two days earlier suffered the same fate.

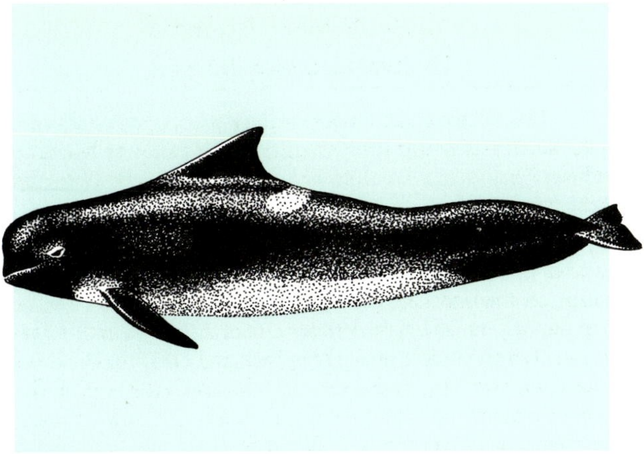

ROUGH-TOOTHED DOLPHIN
(Steno bredanensis)

The large eyes and cone-shaped head of this mammal give it a reptilian appearance. The melon does not have the rounded shape typical of dolphins, but slopes evenly to the tip of the snout.

DESCRIPTION: The flippers of these mammals are large and the dorsal fin quite tall. Most rough-toothed dolphins (the name comes from the numerous fine ridges on their teeth) are about two and a half metres long, give or take a few centimetres. They have dark grey backs, tails, flippers and dorsal fins, paler grey flanks and bellies which are pinkish-white. The lips too are usually white. Scars, possibly caused by cookie-cutter sharks, decorate the body. These 50 centimetre long sharks will brazenly attack larger animals and gouge out their flesh with razor-sharp teeth.

STATUS AND DISTRIBUTION: Found throughout tropical and subtropical areas, rough-toothed dolphins inhabit deeper waters beyond the continental shelf. Strandings of itinerant individuals do occasionally occur in temperate waters. Rough-toothed dolphins are thought to be uncommon. Small numbers are killed for food in some parts of the world. Three were stranded on Barrow Island, offshore from Dampier, in 1971.

LIFE HISTORY: Squid, octopuses and fish form the bulk of their diet. Rough-toothed dolphins tend to live in groups of 50 or less, but are sometimes seen in groups of more than 100. They may also associate with pilot whales, bottlenose dolphins and other dolphin species.

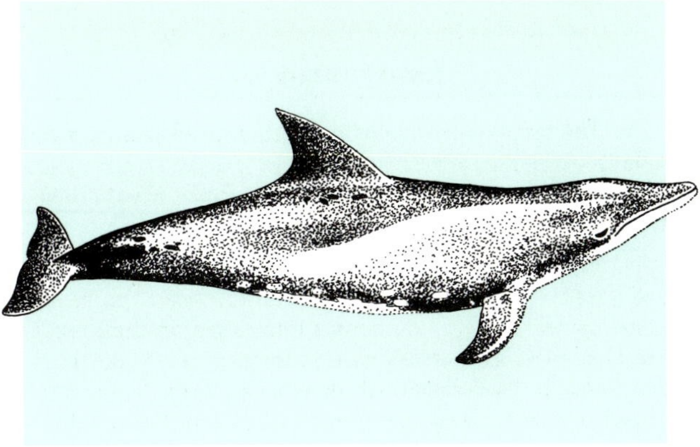

INDO-PACIFIC HUMPBACKED DOLPHIN
(Sousa chinensis)

The most obvious feature of these dolphins is their crookedly humped dorsal fin, which is wide at the base, then flattens out before rising to a triangular, pointed tip. Indo-Pacific humpbacked dolphins hug the shorelines in the primarily tropical waters where they are found. They are rarely seen beyond the surf zone, favouring shallow waters no deeper than 20 metres. They also live in mangrove channels, bays and estuaries.

DESCRIPTION: The maximum length is less than three metres. The colour of these animals varies with age and area, but those in Australia darken to a lead grey colour as they age. The undersides are, however, off-white and the dorsal fin may be white in older animals. The tail is relatively large and the beak is long and slender.

STATUS AND DISTRIBUTION: Though largely tropical, the Indo-Pacific humpbacked dolphin is found in some subtropical areas in association with warm currents. Because of its coastal habits, this dolphin species may be caught accidentally in fishing nets and drowned. Its habitat is also being destroyed or degraded in some areas, for example, reclamation of mangroves. However, the species is not considered threatened.

LIFE HISTORY: Humpbacked dolphins may form loose associations of two or more, but it seems they will readily leave these groups to associate with different animals. These small groups sometimes combine to form larger schools. Humpbacked dolphins feed on a range of schooling fish. A remarkable phenomenon occurs in an area of north-western Africa. When fishermen slap sticks on the water, a number of dolphins arrive to herd the fish into nets and are rewarded with part of the catch. They are slow swimmers but may be seen leaping, chasing or back somersaulting. They rarely bow ride and generally avoid boats.

WHERE TO SEE THEM: They are frequently seen in the Ningaloo Marine Park off the North-West Cape.

IRRAWADDY DOLPHIN
(Orcaella brevirostris)

Scientists only discovered Irrawaddy dolphins in Australia in 1948, although they formed part of the diet of Aboriginal people. Though it is a dolphin, this blunt-headed creature is externally most similar to the beluga whale of the northern hemisphere. Unlike the beluga it is a warm water lover, found in shallow, coastal waters of the tropics and subtropics. Some also live in fresh water, inhabiting rivers with muddy and brackish waters. Although they are quite inconspicuous, they have been known to jump, spy hop and slap their tails.

DESCRIPTION: Irrawaddy dolphins have fairly long flippers with a blowhole set to the left of their heads and no beak. There is a small and quite rounded dorsal fin and a distinct indentation and crease around the neck, which is quite mobile. They are usually greyish-blue, but darker above and lighter below and reach about two and a half metres long.

LIFE HISTORY: Found in groups of up to six and sometimes up to 15, they feed on fish, squid and crustaceans.

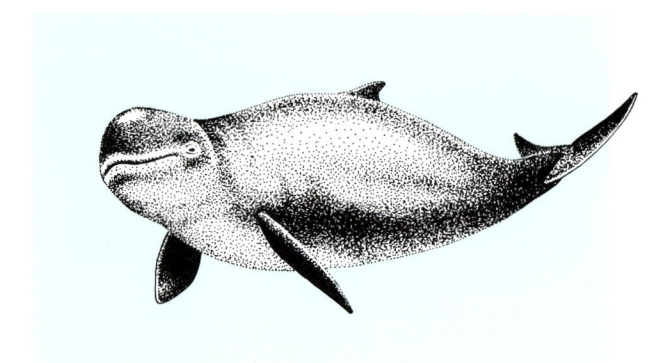

FRASER'S DOLPHIN
(Lagenodelphis hosei)

Fraser's dolphins are quite easily distinguished by their striking markings, their extremely short beaks, the chubby shape of their bodies, small pointed flippers and small triangular dorsal fins. A dark grey stripe masks the eyes and runs the length of the body, further accentuated by cream stripes above and below.

DESCRIPTION: The back, fin, flippers and tail flukes are grey or brownish-blue. They reach a maximum length of little more than two and a half metres. At birth, they are less than a metre long.

STATUS AND DISTRIBUTION: This deep water species is found throughout tropical areas, although three stranded in distinctly cooler waters off Victoria in 1978. Fraser's dolphins appear to be less abundant than several other tropical oceanic dolphins, though in places like the Philippines they are common. Though they are occasionally caught, the population is probably not greatly affected.

LIFE HISTORY: Fraser's dolphins feed on a large variety of fish, crustaceans and squid, and form herds of at least 100. They often mix with other whales and dolphins.

STRANDING HISTORY: An individual became stranded at Samson Point, 30 kilometres north of Karratha, in November 1994 but died soon afterwards.

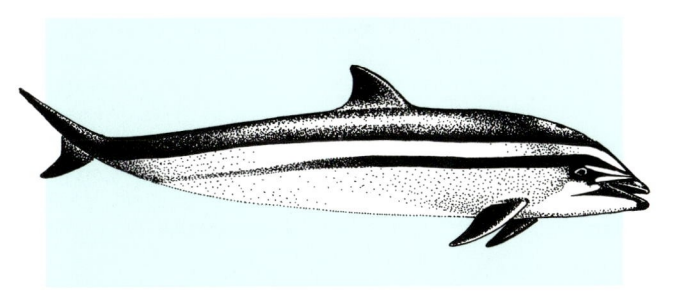

COMMON DOLPHIN
(Delphinus delphis)

People who have visited the Knossos Palace in Crete or seen pictures of the dolphin fresco painted by ancient Minoans will be familiar with the common dolphin. These boisterous mammals seem to enjoy bow riding, breaching and somersaulting clean through the air.

DESCRIPTION: Common dolphins have an hourglass pattern of light grey and tan or yellow on their sides and a dark stripe from flipper to lower jaw, with a long well-defined black beak. Calves display the same patterns but are lighter in colour. They have a prominent triangular dorsal fin, pointed flippers and a slender, streamlined body. Average length varies according to the location, but is approximately two metres.

STATUS AND DISTRIBUTION: These predominantly offshore inhabitants are one of the world's most abundant dolphin species. They are widely distributed throughout tropical, subtropical and temperate areas. They are, however, fished in Japan, South America and elsewhere, depleting some local populations.

LIFE HISTORY: Common dolphins are highly vocal and produce a range of clicks and whistles used for both communication and navigation. They live in large herds, ranging from dozens to more than 1000, which may be segregated according to sex and life cycle. They often combine to catch a variety of prey, favouring squid and smaller schooling fish. Movements are probably related to seasons and offshore banks where upwelling provides better feeding opportunities.

STRANDING HISTORY: Where they strand, common dolphins are usually alone - although one large group stranded in Tasmania in 1975. Strandings in southern California are believed to be caused by parasitic worms damaging brains and ear cavities.

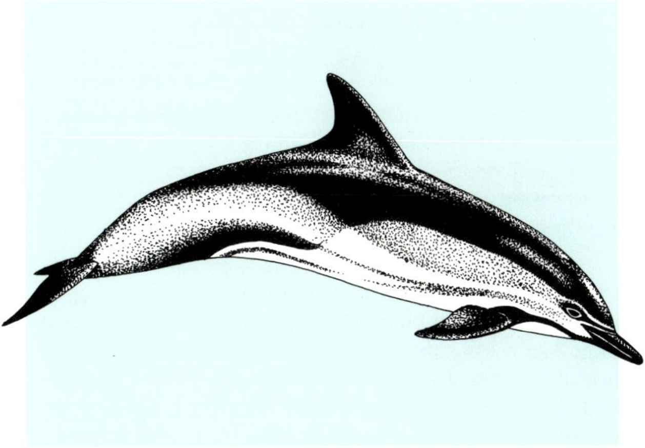

BOTTLENOSE DOLPHIN
(Tursiops truncatus)

The famous dolphins of Monkey Mia are bottlenose dolphins. The Monkey Mia dolphins are wild but regularly visit the shore to interact with people. Bottlenose dolphins are often seen riding on the bow wave created by boats, surfing waves or leaping playfully into the air.

DESCRIPTION: Bottlenose dolphins have prominent dorsal fins, which are seen slicing through the water. The fin is slightly hooked and set midway along the body. This frequently photographed mammal is also easily recognised by its well-formed melon and short, wide and rounded beak. The species has a medium grey back above a pale or light grey flank or belly. The flippers are broad at the base and taper to a point. Bottlenose dolphins are very variable in size, ranging from between two to four metres as adults, depending on where they are found. The Shark Bay population, for instance, is quite small compared to animals seen in Perth waters. Average length is three metres and calves are about a metre at birth.

STATUS AND DISTRIBUTION: This species is common in cold, temperate and tropical seas and estuaries all over the world. It is often seen close inshore in estuaries, even entering rivers, and an offshore form is found in the open ocean. In some parts of the world bottlenose dolphins are killed for food.

LIFE HISTORY: Bottlenose dolphins have a fascinating social structure. Within a population, they form small subgroups which inhabit a defined home range. Members of a group, however, change from time to time and they assist each other in activities such as fish herding and calf rearing. Even mating is a group activity - the males co-operate to herd a female in reproductive condition and take turns to mate with her. They also try to prevent rival groups from having access to her. A calf is generally born 12 months later. The species lives for 25 to 30 years and females begin to breed from about six years of age, calving every two or three years. The calves suckle for up to 18 months. Bottlenose dolphins eat a wide variety of fish, squid and octopuses. The offshore form may be able to dive to depths of more than 600 metres to catch food.

STRANDING HISTORY: Bottlenose dolphins often strand, either singly or in small groups. In October 1990, 11 bottlenose dolphins were returned to the Peel Inlet after becoming trapped in a shallow inland lake and shallow rivers near Mandurah. A major concern when they strand is the risk of sunburn and many animals carry scars from burning.

RISSO'S DOLPHIN
(Grampus griseus)

Risso's dolphins have a white anchor-shaped patch on their chest. Adult animals are otherwise grey over most of their bodies, which are covered with numerous scars and scratches. Older animals may have so many scars that they appear almost white. Risso's dolphins feed mostly on squid but also eat fish. The squid are probably responsible for many of their scars.

DESCRIPTION: Their blunt, square heads have no beak. The mouth slants upward and the front of the melon has a vertical groove. Other features include long, sickle-shaped flippers and a sizeable dorsal fin. They are between three and four metres long when fully grown. Newborn calves are approximately one and a half metres long.

STATUS AND DISTRIBUTION: Risso's dolphins are reasonably widespread and abundant in tropical, subtropical and temperate waters well offshore. Small numbers are fished in various parts of the world, but this probably does not affect numbers to any great extent.

LIFE HISTORY: These mammals live in stable subgroups of a dozen or more, but sometimes form herds of several hundred. The species may associate with other dolphins. Three wild dolphins thought to be hybrids, born as a result of breeding between Risso's dolphins and bottlenose dolphins, have been recorded. They may swim side-by-side in formations known as "chorus lines" and will spy hop, breach and slap their tails and flippers. Sounds such as whistles are probably used to communicate.

STRANDING HISTORY: Individual and mass strandings occur throughout the species' range.

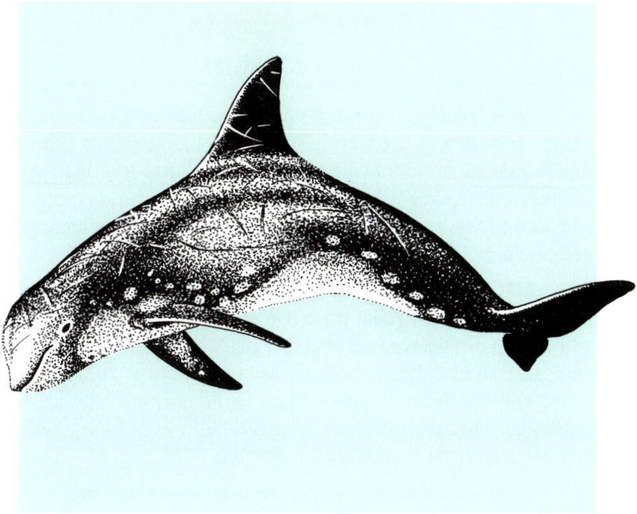

SPOTTED DOLPHIN
(Stenella attenuata)

Spotted dolphins are found in tropical and subtropical oceans throughout the world. They seem to enjoy bow riding, flipping forward and lobbing their tails, and may leap high out of the water. The species is more likely to inhabit the open ocean and seems to favour low saline waters with surface temperatures greater than 25 degrees Celcius.

DESCRIPTION: Spotted dolphins are light grey, with a dark grey cape. They may reach up to two and a half metres long. The white spots on these animals become bigger and more numerous with age, and newborn dolphins have no spots at all. Coastal forms are heavily spotted, but those found offshore have fewer markings. This species has a relatively tall fin and long beak, and older animals may develop white lips.

STATUS AND DISTRIBUTION: Thousands are killed every year as a result of tuna fishing. They are also taken directly in Japan and the Solomon Islands. Although their numbers have been reduced as a result, they are still very common.

LIFE HISTORY: Spotted dolphins often associate with spinner dolphins and flocks of feeding seabirds and yellowfin tuna (and are therefore used by tuna fishermen to locate their catches). They feed on squid, flying fish and other fish in surface waters. Schools range in size from a few dozen to several thousand and these may be segregated by age, sex and reproductive status. They may live for as long as 45 years. Although they are not known to migrate, tagged animals have been recorded moving up to 2400 kilometres.

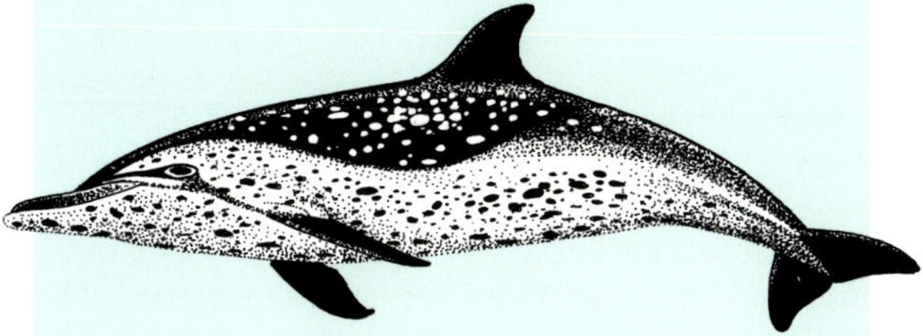

STRIPED DOLPHIN
(*Stenella coeruleoalba*)

Striped dolphins are active, playful and distinctively patterned. They are most often seen in large schools and one of these stranded at Augusta in 1989, before most were returned to the ocean by rescuers. A school of more than 1000 was reported off Geraldton in 1979.

DESCRIPTION: This dolphin is distinguished by a dark stripe running from flipper to eye, and from the eye to the end of the body. It is bluish-grey on top and has a white belly with lighter grey sides. A shoulder blaze curves up from above and behind the flippers towards the dorsal fin. Adults may reach about three and a half metres long, while calves are about a metre at birth.

STATUS AND DISTRIBUTION: This species lives offshore and is rarely seen in coastal waters. It is reasonably common and is widely distributed across all temperate, subtropical and tropical seas. Off Japan, they have been hunted for centuries.

LIFE HISTORY: Striped dolphins feed on lanternfish and other fish species, squid and shrimps. They live in large groups, usually numbering between 100 and 500, with juveniles, mating adults (along with their calves) and non-mating adults living in separate groups. Juveniles leave the adult group when weaned, at about 18 months, and rejoin an adult group when they become sexually mature (between five and nine years for both males and females). They often leap from the water and bow ride. They vocalise with clicks and whistles. Off Japan they migrate in association with a warm current.

STRANDING HISTORY: Strandings of individuals are reasonably common but mass strandings are rare. In January 1989, 24 striped dolphins stranded at Augusta.

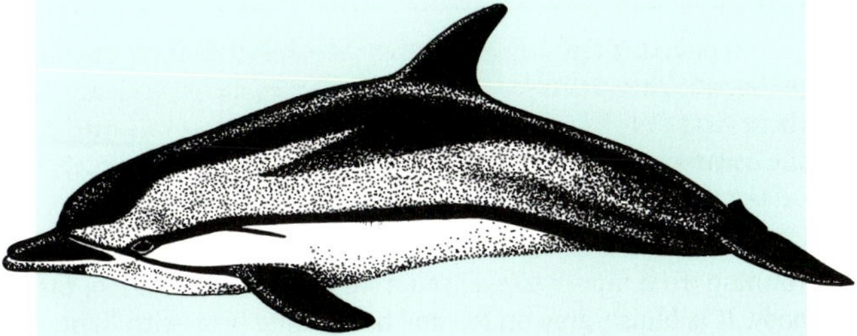

SHORE SURVIVORS

Strandings of marine mammals - many of them single animals - occur much more frequently than most people realise along the extensive coastline of WA. Sometimes, certain species of whales and dolphins beach themselves in large numbers. The Department of Conservation and Land Management (CALM) is responsible for conserving the wildlife of WA, and CALM wildlife officers are usually the first people called to a stranding. Over the last few years, CALM wildlife officers have developed considerable expertise and a high success rate when dealing with marine mammal strandings.

During supervised rescues, great care is taken to carry the animals gently in a sling, clear of any snags, as they could become vulnerable to infection if the skin is broken. Handling a whale or dolphin the wrong way can cause it distress, and even damage the tissue or internal organs.

RESEARCH: At each stranding, valuable information is collected for use in research. Each animal is temporarily tagged, numbered, measured and sexed. A vet checks their condition and takes blood samples. The samples are later analysed to see if the animals are dehydrated or have abnormal levels of hormones or enzymes in their blood due to stress. CALM wildlife officers freeze-brand the animals by immersing a brand in liquid nitrogen and holding it against the skin - a painless process. The marks may remain for more than 20 years, making it possible to identify any animals that are resighted or restranded, giving valuable information on how long they survive and whether they are behaving in a normal way.

SAFETY: Safety is a major concern at strandings. Whales and dolphins are powerful animals, and the rescuers themselves could be bitten or hit by the tail. Conditions at the site are often cold, wet and hazardous.

EUTHANASIA: If the animal is suffering and a vet advises that there is no doubt that it will die, even if returned to the wild, the animal is euthanased. This is only done if it is the most humane option.

VOLUNTEERS: CALM often calls in volunteers from groups such as Westwhales and Greenpeace to provide the personpower needed to conduct a successful rescue. CALM conducts regular workshops to train members of these groups in marine mammal rescue techniques. Anyone interested in helping at future rescues should join one of these groups.

For more information, or to advise of a stranding, contact the Department of Conservation and Land Management, 50 Hayman Road, Como on (09) 334 0292. To advise of a stranding emergency after hours phone (09) 334 0224, (09) 401 8183 or (09) 401 2823.

SIGHTING RECORD

SPECIES	DATE	LOCALITY	REMARKS
southern right whale			
pygmy right whale			
blue whale			
Bryde's whale			
minke whale			
humpback whale			
sperm whale			
pygmy sperm whale			
dwarf sperm whale			
Arnoux's beaked whale			
southern bottlenose whale			
Cuvier's beaked whale			
Shepherd's beaked whale			
Blainville's beaked whale			
True's beaked whale			
straptoothed whale			
scamperdown whale			

SIGHTING RECORD

SPECIES	DATE	LOCALITY	REMARKS
Andrew's beaked whale			
melon-headed whale			
pygmy killer whale			
false killer whale			
killer whale			
long-finned pilot whale			
short-finned pilot whale			
rough-toothed dolphin			
Indo-Pacific humpbacked dolphin			
Irrawaddy dolphin			
Fraser's dolphin			
common dolphin			
bottlenose dolphin			
Risso's dolphin			
spotted dolphin			
striped dolphin			

INDEX

Andrew's beaked whale	33
Arnoux's beaked whale	25
Blainville's beaked whale	29
blue whale	12-13
bottlenose dolphin	52-53
Bryde's whale	14-15
common dolphin	50-51
Cuvier's beaked whale	27
dwarf sperm whale	24
false killer whale	36-37
Fraser's dolphin	49
humpback whale	17-19
Indo-Pacific humpbacked dolphin	46-47
Irrawaddy dolphin	48
killer whale	38-39
long-finned pilot whale	40-41
melon-headed whale	34
minke whale	16
pygmy killer whale	35
pygmy right whale	10-11
pygmy sperm whale	23
Risso's dolphin	54-55
rough-toothed dolphin	44-45
scamperdown whale	32
Shepherd's beaked whale	28
short-finned pilot whale	42-43
southern bottlenose whale	26
southern right whale	6-9
sperm whale	20-22
spotted dolphin	56-57
striped dolphin	58-59
straptoothed whale	31
True's beaked whale	30

4160-0196-12500